DO THE RIGHT THING!

KINDNESS

Written by Diane Muldrow
Illustrated by Mary O'Keefe Young

ROURKE BOOK CO., INC.
VERO BEACH, FL 32964

Printed in the United States of America.

Library of Congress Cataloging-in-Publication Data

Muldrow, Diane.
    Kindness / Diane Muldrow.
        p.   cm. — (Doing the right thing)
  Summary: Examines the nature and importance of kindness and how it can be expressed.
    ISBN 1-55916-233-3
    1. Kindness—Juvenile literature. [1. Kindness.]   I. Title.
II. Series.
BJ1533.K5M85   1999
177.7—dc21   98-48390
                                                            CIP
                                                           AC

KINDNESS

What is kindness?

Kindness is being gentle, loving, and helpful to others. It is kind to share your sandwich with your friend who forgot his lunch.

Kindness is a friendly smile to welcome
the new kid who is feeling all alone.

6

Kindness is letting a frog
you have caught go free.

You can be kind to a plant by
watering it.

You can be kind to a cat by
not teasing it.

When you share the last piece of
pumpkin pie with your little brother,
you are being kind.

Kindness is not laughing when somebody
drops a tray in the cafeteria.

You are being kind when you choose
for your team the kid who is never
chosen until last.

Kindness is often about sharing.
Kindness is sharing your umbrella
on a rainy day.

Kindness is lending a helping a hand.

Kindness is giving clothes and toys
you do not need any longer to someone
who has less than you have.

Sometimes kindness is about listening.

Kindness is helping around the house
when your mom feels sick.

Kindness is making your friend laugh
when she has been crying over her
bad haircut.

Kindness is helping someone learn
something new.

27

Sometimes kindness is just being there for someone.

Be kind to others, and they
will be kind to you.

You Can Be Kind!

These steps can help you be kind. But do NOT write in this book; use a sheet a paper.

1. **Choose ways to be kind.** Write 6 ways, like these:
    Smile at someone who looks lonely.
    Listen to a friend who is sad or angry.
    Give my baby toys to a clinic.
    Stroke a kitten or puppy.
    Fix a broken toy for the kid next door.
    Show my little sister how to draw.

2. **Choose who you can be kind to.** Write 6 names. Then write 6 more.

sister	dad	janitor	clerk
stranger	buddy	bus driver	pet

3. **Choose how to be kind to each person.** After each name, write a way to be kind. Use your list or think of new ways.

sister	Listen when she's angry.
clerk	Smile and say "thanks."
buddy	Help with schoolwork.

4. **Choose to start now.** Be kind to someone before you go to bed tonight.

5. **Choose to be kind each day.** Think about kindness soon after you get out of bed.

6. **Write these words every evening:**
    Today I was kind to _____. My kindness was _____.
Fill in the blanks. Use the same paper every time. Keep it up for 2 weeks or more.

7. **Say, "I am a kind person."**
    Say it many times every day.